Rebekah Ord
Lasagna

Rebekah Orders
Lasagna

Poems by
John Jenkinson

Preface by Bruce Bond
Editor: Eleanor Bell

Rebekah Orders Lasagna
Copyright 2006 by John Jenkinson
International Standard Book Number 0-939391-38-4

Manufactured in the United States of America
Woodley Press
Washburn University
Topeka, Kansas 66621
All Rights Reserved

First Edition

Cover photo: Nicholas Dryden
Author photo: photo machine, Gare du Nord, Paris, France
Model: Rebekah Dryden
Cover design: Nicholas Dryden, John Jenkinson
Book design: Roberta Sheahan

Acknowledgments

Thanks to the readers and editors in whose journals these poems first appeared, sometimes slightly altered:

American Literary Review, "Vernal Equinox," "The Dim Estate," "Earth as a Place of Burial"
Envision, "How to Get Married," "How Domenica Lazzari Survived on Light," "The August Patio," "Visiting a River Valley Town," "What the Table-dancer Earned"
Georgia Review, "Why Orville and Wilbur Built an Airplane"
Grasslands Review, "Rain"
Hiram Poetry Review, "Indulgences"
Illya's Honey, "Honey"
Iron Horse, "Lullaby"
Kansas Voices 2, "The Kites"
New Journal, "Rehearsal"
North Texas Review, "What the Loon Believes"
Passages North, "The History of Sleep," "The Shallows," "Lot's Daughters," "King's Harlot to Rook One"
Portland Review, "Watching 'The Invisible Man'"
Poetry for the Masses, "Circus Girl," "Trimming the Dead"
Quarterly West, "South of Red-Wing"
Raintown Review, "Grandfather's Republic"
Rattle, "The Way Light Gets to Be"
Seems, "Barns"
Shocker Magazine, "Abandon"
Sulphur River Literary Review, "Picnic with Guitar"
32 Poems, "Waiting," "Canapés"
Tumbleweed Review, "The Kites"
Visions International, "Resolution" (as "Two in a Bush")
Windhover, "The Shalene Tree"
Writers Bloc, "The Bee of Hearts"

Acknowledgments

"South of Red-Wing" received an AWP Intro/Journals Award.
"Honey" received a Dallas Poet's Community Award.
"The Kites" received a Kansas Voices Award
"The Kites" appears in the anthology *Kansas Voices III* (WAHC, 2004).
"The Way Light Gets to Be" appears in the anthology *Alchemical Proofs*, Marie C. Jones and Jean Roelke, eds. (Denton: Basilisk, 2002), and the *Sheridan-Edwards Review*, slightly altered.
"Why Orville and Wilbur Built an Airplane" was reprinted, slightly revised, in *The Mennonite*, with permission.
"Lullaby" was reprinted, slightly altered, in *The Shocker*, with permission.
Several of these poems appear in the chapbook *The History of Sleep* (Denton: Basilisk, 2002).
"Rebekah Orders Lasagna" appears in monograph: PCA/ACA Annual Joint Conference, 2004.

Special thanks to The Milton Center for a post-doctoral Poetry Fellowship during which some of these poems were composed or amended, and to the Milton Center Writers' Workshop members for their generous critique and attention. Thank you Essie Sappenfield, Lise Goett, and Bryan Dietrich.

Thanks also to the ad hoc writers group (Cathy Jenkinson, Lisa Moser, Peg Flynn, Mary Seitz, Laura Stangel-Schmidt, Melissa Stanton, Barbara Stewart, Jack Wessels) for their love and patience.

Deepest gratitude for the many teachers, colleagues, students, and friends who have guided, and continue to guide me, through a preposterous life.

And a deep bow to Madeline DeFrees, Debora Greger, David Huddle, Eric Pankey, John Poch, Henry Taylor, and Lee Young-Li, for helpful readings of these, as well as other, poems. And . . .

The Basilisk ladies, Marie C. Jones and Jean Roelke, for their faith;

The Woodley gang, for their belief and good offices;

The students, staff, faculty, and administration of Butler Community College for their generous moral, emotional, and financial support of my endeavors.

And love to my blurbers, whose public testimony on my behalf testifies to their own deep generosity.

Finally, God bless Yevgeny Yevtushenko for "the kiss."

*For my wife, Cathy,
and our wildly extended family*

In memory

*Jill Snapp
C. Walden Dye
J.B. Jenkinson*

Contents

A Dim Estate
Earth as a Place of Burial	3
South of Red Wing	5
Lullaby	6
Rehearsal	7
Trimming the Dead	9
Picnic with Guitar	10
Rites of Damage	11
A Dim Estate	13
Barns	14
The Shalene Tree	15
Abandon	17

The Happy Family
How to Get Married	21
Rain	22
Grandfather's Republic	23
Why Orville and Wilbur Built an Airplane	25
Watching "The Invisible Man"	26
The Way Light Gets to Be	29
The August Patio	31
Visiting A River Valley Town	32
Rebekah Orders Lasagna	33

Lovebirds and Other Fish
The Shallows	41
What the Loon Believes	42
Lot's Daughters	43
King's Harlot to Rook One	44
What the Table-dancer Earned	45
Circus Girl	46
Indulgences	47
How Domenica Lazzari Survives on Light	48
The Bee of Hearts	49
Honey	50
The Kites	51
Waiting	52
Vernal Equinox	53
The History of Sleep	54
Canapés	56
Resolution	57

Preface

The world of John Jenkinson's debut volume of poetry is enormous. Everywhere we turn in these poems we meet the spirit of generosity and invention, the resourcefulness of an imagination that routinely gestures toward the everyday while refusing the ordinary, refusing an easy posture of repose. Everywhere we turn we meet another feast, a verbal abundance at times Hopkinsesque, at times both reverent and audacious, at times both homage to and embodiment of the transformative powers of nature. That these powers are forboding in places is palpable enough, giving the book its soulfulness and heft. That they also occasion praise is part of the great blessing of a mind always eager for the next animating surprise, the next joke or tune to cheer us, the next sweet sting of loss making way for the new.

Moreover, the flourishes of imagination here are so consistent and lush that they make conspicuous the paradox of all good poetry, that it both embraces and competes with the real, that its metaphors speak a truth that is half-discovered, half-forged. Thus this great love-hate relationship with the real. Thus this work that eschews both the dreariness of a flatter realism and the frivolity of uncommitted fancy. The trick is arriving at a kind of precision of inwardness, a voice authenticated both by its witness and its freedom. (Too much irony can kill a book. Or too little.) Suffice it to say that the freedom here is daring indeed, far more so than you would expect from a first volume. Or if you were to find such audacity of reach in a new poet, it is rarer still to find it wedded to such authority, such gravity and craft.

This is not to say that a certain density of line and diction in this collection takes itself too seriously. Far from it. The very title Rebekah Orders Lasagna points to the quotidian plenitude of the book, yes, but handled with a lively tonal suppleness. This suppleness is one more face of generosity and abundance, another face of freedom. If the lasagna here is a thick meal, it is also peppered with wit and a lightness of touch. Part of the inviting complexity in the work stems from a tumbling syntax that gets refreshed by humor, wicked candor, and emphatic concision. If some anticipated decorum is broken in the process, so be it. The shattering of such decorum figures as a sign of spontaneity and play, a sign of the living voice. And that voice becomes so essential, so welcome in dressing down the more formidable aspects of style.

One more face of generosity in this book is its tremendous music, the attention to form, to the sensuous breathing of melody and rhythm. While it is true that many of the lines here are so finely chiseled they could cut glass, it is equally true that they have the ever fading and renewing beauty of song. While so many contemporary poets have abandoned the preeminence of music in their work, Mr. Jenkinson remains rooted in the fertile tradition of the lyric. The result is lines that have both integrity of the well-made thing and the elusiveness of something sung and fleeting. And not one line is wasted. For this and for the many pleasures to be found in this book, I am deeply grateful. It is with this gratitude that I trust this volume will find its honored place in the world, that it will make its way into the hearts of readers and expand.

–Bruce Bond

Let wise men piece the world together with wisdom
    Or poets with holy magic.
  Hey-di-ho.

—Wallace Stevens

A Dim Estate

Ay; or else 'twere hard luck, being in so preposterous estate as we are.

— William Shakespeare,
The Winter's Tale V. ii

Earth as a Place of Burial

In brindled file, the Herefords, Angus amble
loose-muscled, heavy boned, and plump
with the Flint Hills' fading grasses,
as we loll at the barbed fence-line,
a clutch of broad-brimmed flowers
shooting the breeze around the weed stems
wedged between our teeth.

The cattle disregard our teeth.
Mothers curl their thick, pink tongues
against the matted calf fur
even though the calves stand near
full growth themselves and chew their cud
with a leisure known to those for whom
desire is just another bull beyond a fence.

Easing to yellow, bluestem battens
down another summer. A choke
of sumac bleeds along the creek, where woods
gnarl up in gold and mixed siennas,
the lime-green snap of hedgeapples,
grapevine's tough gray twist.

The world stumbles
into its slow season as manure steams
an age-old sweetness
across the pasture's hoof-pocked surface
into morning's hesitant frost.

Someone from the food chain glistens—
a bag of bloodied leather
emptied in a carnage of bottlebrush

where the meadow meets the trees.
This is what we remember of the night,
what the brooding herd repeats.

Jigging her bell in the morning haze,
the lead cow tolls what winter promises—
dormant frogs in mud;
the death of grain;
our earth a hard and frozen thing;
farm dogs and the loading ramp.

South of Red-Wing

I wake up on the wrong side of the equinox,
geese in isosceles stitches
trace a path down the world's face, stop
to ravish the harvest's sun-dried trash

piled in furrows and hedgerows.
A clatter of crows pleats the air
with black derision, brushes a red-wing
off the taut wire of her discretion.

Summer's long truce broken, the mice
have returned to the catfood, gnawed
dank passage to that heavy yellow sack,
peppered our floor with their delicate scat.

This bounty of need, feeling
the leaves crack as the cat stalks
his own red meal, whiskers his way
through the crisp buffalo grass.

Something has burrowed into the half-assed
pumpkin patch—skunk, badger,
another hair-shirt mendicant
telling her beads along the food chain,

clicking the beetles' lacquer-thin shells,
snapping brittle seed-hulls
in her frowsty cell, far from the sun's ache,
taking no thought for the morrow.

Thin fires kiss the evenings now
beneath the railway trestle; and the men
with cardboard signs, trolling the highways
in denim and flannel, all drift south.

Lullaby

> a person is a narrative, /the strength of which is either /revelation or withholding.
> —*Albert Goldbarth*

Sweet with mildew and leaf-rot,
a choked pump-filter chugs the same slow song
that plays where grout splits,
where nail rust roots in powdering latex,
where an Oldsmobile blossoms in oxides
under a wrestle of hedge-gnarl and ivy, sinks
to its ferrous knees in a wrangle of clover and bullthistle—
or where a human hair traces its long fall
from scalp to brush bristle, to linoleum.

I sip coffee and watch as Miranda tidies
her house, attacks the tatted spiderweb binding her
ceiling to her wall, sweeps a battered feather
duster over her well-thumbed books,
then asks herself, out loud, what she has learned
that a cornstraw broom couldn't
have taught in half the time.

Matter scuffs in the corners of rooms—tumbleweeds
of cat fur snowy with dust, mouse Braille, lacy flakes
of forgotten skin—the teeming caboodle of life
slipping away to a quiet place . . .
under the broken patio tiles, in a shimmer
of nacreous clay, gray slugs repose.

What kind of thing do her children think her?
Soft in the head as firelight
chewing a summer's fallen twigs.
A husband dawdles in the garden
shed with turf-rouged rakes and hoes.

From a back-room radio, Stan Getz whispers Desafinado
over a drummer's bossa-nova brushes.
She turns to me, lifts her coffee cup in a modest toast.
At last, she says, she's turned
a kind of beetle, her home a carapace
grown difficult to bear, the surfaces smoky
with the patina of long use—
and everything she used to be?
A thumb-smudge pledged to one last varnished door.

Rehearsal

1.
Below the rustling olive leaves
Andre bends his head to the soundboard,
intent as a shoemaker's apprentice
or a mapmaker charting new terrain.
The high strings drill their freezing rivulet
into a stony audience, chill
the smoky haze that lusters,
ghostly, between the hand-spaced trees.

From every tricky fugue, from each ornate
fandango with an Arabic devotion
to the minor keys, he's stolen
some hard kernel which he sows
into those furrows blind winds
gouge in darkening air.

2.
His mother and his daughter still aspire
to taste Grenada's concert season,
to unfold, bold blossoms on the velvet plush,
awash in rhapsody and gilt
as Andre tenders his guitar, not like a woman
asleep in his arms, but like a pet
that growls between the notes.

As sundown sinks into the stone-
walled common well,
the younger village women congregate.
He resolves the tune for how they mill,
purring rumors and romances
while they smother in their families
and tend their bearded bands of tinkling goats.

3.
As if the concert hall his fingertips
imagine thrills in tandem
with the well's cool depths
or the obsidian eyes these gypsy women
roll to greet his chordal substitutions,
Andre shuts his eyes against a world
of callused palms, of scythes and shovels,
plows and plowings,
of cuttings-down and buryings.

His last full notes attenuate
as evening's raiment of birds rehearse
the slightest touch of light on feather, serenade
his mother's black-clad figure dipping water,
the sunset fading from her arm
and slipping fret to fret across his daughter.

Trimming the Dead

Sweating through his t-shirt, my father broils
beneath the atmosphere's convex lens
and squats in the front garden, retired
on his haunches among the flags,
trimming the dead
shoots, the dry husks, the curls
of yellowed leaves
furling their decaying promises.

Bowed beneath a pale straw hat
his Labrador retrieved and gnawed
to something like a haystack,
he's ducking sunstroke and painting,
he supposes, the very air
above the iris bed with Forbidden Fruit's
persimmon orange, Blushing Duchess,
peachblow soft as love.

His next door neighbor's daughter
walks her Pekinese, smiles and waves
at his labor. She's budding
out this summer, too, and boys
surround her every evening,
a cloud of sizzling bees who pay
with stolen honey for each buzz and sting
creaked on her front-porch swing.

As finely honed as knives, he thinks—
the tools of pruning; he must watch
himself. He nipped a fingertip
last season, daydreaming, and learned
firsthand to cultivate his fantasies
in real dirt. Surrounded by mounds
of discarded flower-flesh, he rises, stiffly,
bearing a dead bouquet in his arms.

Picnic with Guitar

The string murmurs . . . and still, the string forgets.
    Harmonics flatten, fail, the way my brief prayers
stink the shore of Raccoon Creek this rocky
    afternoon. My wife, who lives to root
beneath the scenery, puts on a boot
    she's scavenged from a tangle of debris.
Whose bulrush basket brims with nosegay and knuckles?

The blues I pick to pluck don't cheer her feet.
    She rides me like an ass through thorns and troubles
to where the blue-black berries swell, where heat
    compels the chiggers to our naked ankles.
She hops on one leg as I load a plastic
    bucket full of fruit, lug it, straining,
to our picnic spot. My hands feel stained.

With brazen wine! Hard seeds we cannot eat!
    She may be mad. I may forget to bleed her.
By way of luring leeches who can kiss
    her flesh like Doctor Nazarene, I fall
and lave my wretched face with dirt. Dire names
    the Jesus cantor dares not breathe, she chants—
and even now, the universe of chance

rubs like an old, familiar cat against
    her retina, wipes away the sticky light
that cleaves to her. A blackbird lifts her song
    as a red-tail stoops, many-feathered-lightning,
to gig an inattentive vole. Across
    the stream, I swear, a puppet child on strings
beats unsuspecting air with vinyl wings.

A rubber hot-dog and a loaf of rye!
    A pound of prickled gooseflesh packed in brine . . .
I never understand what wild birds cry,
    or how they bury tunes within their bones
unto a thousandth hollow generation.
    Gnawing on the blackberries we savor,
we ripple our small marriage in the river.

Rites of Damage

Now, grown old and crapulous,
   I celebrate the dead
      in pious cliché,
   and wear their underclothes,
smuggled out of second-hand stores
      beneath my shirt
as the clerk demurely looks the other way.
I spend my life in other peoples' stains.

My cousin's suits hang with the others
   against the long back wall
      like ironed cadavers.
   The flesh fell from his bones
like feathers from a molting bird
      in those last months.
And though I visited, he knew I'd rather
hit the bars alone, and let him suffer

privately, indignant, his nurses
   grave and silent tugboats
      bumping him
   slowly out to sea.
And, like him, his fragile ward-mates
      drifted away,
starless, blind with intravenous morphine,
the rites of damage scored with medicine.

They have gone to a better place.
   We live for this assertion,
      like frightened hares
   nibbling on weeds that crane
from newly abandoned flower plots
      to gather sun.
I chew a sprig of Johnson grass and stare
hard across the garden and the years

I've mumbled through my hometown streets,
   anticipate the worst
      from dogs and men.
   My chancy heart stutters.
I cough into a handkerchief—
      a black smitch.
These tongueless two-tone shoes and tapping cane
outpace the shuffling footsteps of my brain.

The dead arrive late at my house
   where a low fire gutters
      in the gas grate
   like the liquid struggle of a chest
heaving its last tough breath.
      I still utter
prayers for them——not like a saint, or Jesus,
but like a man whose neck burns in its noose.

A Dim Estate

We crave the meat within its hull,
   A sweetness in the cask—
A song unsung in unrung bells—
   An image in a glass

That no eye yet has dallied on.
   A *sotto voce* snowfall
Mutes the colors of our town
   With blankness prodigal,

Stanches words we would have said
   Before we crossed to sleep.
The moon on leaden snowfields sheds
   Reflected light, not grief.

Our city's cars are long and black,
   An angel on each hood.
The men who drive are lorn and bleak—
   They never speak a word,

But sip an antique beverage
   Of vinegar and rue—
They wheel us to our acreage—
   A narrow one will do.

Barns

The gambrel-lofted barns, worn siding painted in trade
for advertising (Chew Mail Pouch Tobacco fades
like the veteran who brushed it), fall to their knees
in axles and bundled wire, pigweed's graying
spikes, and bow their hay-points toward autumn dirt.

They haven't a prayer. The new kids on the site
sport galvanized steel sides, corrugate sunlight
as it wiggles its hips across the winter wheat sprouts
west of Garfield. Impervious to drought
or flood, the ravening of weather's appetite,

they stud the tilled and irrigated prairie
fly-specked with huddled little towns where weary
farmers bunch around the Co-op to plan
late fall's erections. City-boys truck the new barns
in, drop them disassembled in the chaff.

But, all barns chew the same cud: honed tools,
new leather, feed sacks—and purge their bowels
of cogwheels, blunt hoes, old spurs' rusty rowels.
Someone waits for love in a half-lit hayloft.
Out behind the barn, the kittens learn to smoke.

The Shalene Tree

> When from the Tree my God was hung
> A thousand Birdes flew from the Woode,
> Their Feathers blacked the very Sunne
> And blotted up the living Bloode.
>
> —*Anon. (c. 1500 C.E.)*

1.
They planted, after their youngest girl
died, an oak. A plaque of marble

beneath the tree told her name
and date. This wrist-thick sapling came,

it seemed, as balm to the Shepherds' neighbors.
That empty Christmas, with great labor,

a boy from next door wired an angel
onto a frosted branch. She dangled

like unyielding ice in the sun's eye,
and over the years that multiply

populations, she has grown
to roughly a dozen rugged, windblown

seraphim who hang from baling
wire and pray for short Shalene.

2.
We bought the place. We hadn't lived
there very long till my wife grieved

for dead Shalene as if she'd lost
the child herself, as if the rest

of us were incomplete, surface
only. She brooded to find peace,

but reached an awkward covenant
and carried home an ornament

to hang among the feathered ones
that grace the sleeping Shalene's bones.

She tied a blown-glass fairy there,
on a golden string in autumn air.

3.
Kicking leaves, I struck a head
beneath the tree, among the dead

that pile below the pin oak's crown.
Her small lips curved a bow—a frown

as pensive as our blue-eyed daughter—
then shook the air with plucky laughter

half-way between the see-saw chatter
jackdaws dither and the first splatter

of freezing rain on window glass.
In this tree, a different class

of critter, angels, fly from wires,
suspended, baled by their desires

for light-bedazzled heavenly things.
When autumn shakes, the last leaf clings.

Their wings are feathered, soft as birds'
that stanched the passion of the Lord;

but hers? Little insect wings
like those that buzz at backdoor screens

when oleanders break in bloom.
Here, the angels made no room

to squeeze a flitting fairy—fey,
and born like girls to fall away.

Abandon

> What about the smell of light?
> What about the moss?
>
> —John Ashbery

You tell me you've never heard it—
the difficult age of things calling
out from the hardpan fields
where stubble and roadgrade collide
in a muddle of loose stones
and tractor prints;
where a couple who parked for an evening
abandoned to love
awaken as cobwebbed skeletons
humming their lies
into the O of a fence-post tire,
its white-washed No Hunting
message surrendering each day
a little more to the sun.
It sounds like a sky
washed clean of birds,
where only the flutter of wings
lingers, or like the spot
where a footprint shivers
down to the molten heart of the earth.

The Happy Family

How happy is the little stone
That rambles in the road alone

—Emily Dickinson

How to Get Married

We declare our love by barking
at the neighbor's dog, and vow
to eat the troubled thing
we've killed. It's Illium
writ small—the intercessions

of minor gods, the smoke
and mirrors as each deception
stands deadpanned on the stage
where our meager history
demands a good excavating.

Even the olive trees rustle and squeak
as you excoriate my venal sins:
tender your mulehide crop,
swash your fervent tongue.
Today a shrill wind grips

the stop signs in its fierce
dry hands and shakes till screws
fall like seeds into the street.
One of them blossoms into the car
in which we drive our honeymoon.

Rain

The weight of rain rings on the window,
blurs our lucid neighborhood
into one soft body dripping
at the edges, the gelid
figures of Monet.

Should we open our roof to this baptist
moment? Hold up our hands to the holy
wash of a passing ghost
who keens in steady half-light? Devote
ourselves to that dogged revision

of a known territory required by our new
Atlas? You still me with a single
finger to your joined lips, gaze
through the mirror our window has become
at the rain's daughters

sweeping the long ground
with gray gowns, walking the way
girls walk who are foolish
with love, muffling the traffic's hiss,
the suddenly important bells.

Grandfather's Republic

The south wind holds him like a raw-boned girl,
burns his ears, then slaps his gaunt cheeks red
and drops him, a ragged, thatch-haired scarecrow propped
where nothing tempts the birds, where low hills thrust
their flint outcroppings through the tangled grama.
He's choked his hard way back to eastern Kansas

from the war, and finds the landscape nothing
like France with its steel-pocked air, the yellow gas
that thickened in the draws while his Springfield
drummed a last tattoo for German youth.
At seventeen, overworked and crazy
with the farm, he swallowed every yarn

the recruiting sergeant dished up to the rubes
of the republic for a stint in meat-lined trenches.
Two winters hunched him down in ice and mud,
but here, spring-bent hackberry jazz their greens
like sizzle-cymbals, toss their minor shrapnel
—unrequited claims, curt promises served

to the dying. Recalling every shade-gray face
that slipped beneath the grass, he hears the brass-clad
cartridge slide in its chamber, the solid clamping
home of the bolt. Toward Elk County, storm clouds
spread and boil frothing vapor over
the sky's blue-dappled pan. This time, he vows

to find a shape to curb the monuments,
to cull the stars that wound the small-town windows
and paste them back into the spendthrift heavens.
A stir of pollen drops him to his knees,
coughing broken penance to the grassheads
as a circling peregrine calls out, declares

the stone rich grazing acreage a half-dead
paradise. And like a cloud, his head
expands to fill the space between his thoughts,
while in the weeds a king snake's dry skin rustles
a trip-wire memory. Alive at last,
Grandfather crafts a new life from the cow bones

in no-man's land, aims to stretch a woman's
skin across the bleached white frame he'll raise
as temple in this wilderness. The storm
bulls closer, forks its lightning tongue above
a small and crippled thing, alone on the prairie,
who jigs as raindrops kick the dust like bullets.

Why Orville & Wilbur Built an Airplane

Life, as we suspected, is a bicycle
lacking a kickstand: pedal
along for a while,

then lay it down. Some
of us glide serenely down
a long, easy hill on three-

pound Italian racers, scarcely
using any of their twenty-two
well-lubricated gears. Others

must dismount to walk
these leaden Western Flyers up
that hot, steep slope, mugged

by heavy corduroys under a midsummer
sun, light from the heavy chrome
fenders kissing our eyes closed,

the bright air that clogs our passage
thickening with effort—the shaky
wire baskets filling with rocks.

Watching 'The Invisible Man'

    —for Marie Jones and Bryan Dietrich

1.
Mom
                burning

                          to see The Invisible

in
          father

       pretends

I see it coming
                          rabid

in chenille houseshoes

2.
Mom peeks up
　　　　while burning
　　　my time
　　　　　　to see The Invisible
　　come into view
in grainy English.
　　　　　My father grins
　　　　a twelve-inch Admiral
　　jokes, but Mom
　　　　pretends she cannot hear
　　　　　another burnt up pig.
　　　　　Dad kicks back a
　　　　　　　　　rabid mink
in chenille houseshoes,　　disappears.

3.
Mom peeks up from our wobbly kitchen table
and wonders aloud, while burning our supper pork loin,
how I'm wasting my time. But I explain
above the TV that I'm here to see The Invisible
Man come into view, if he is able,
in grainy English black and white,— Claude Rains'
invisible debut. My father grins.
He's staring at a twelve-inch Admiral,
he jokes, but Mom, swathed in ribboned smoke,
fusses and pretends she cannot hear.
We don't need another burnt up pig.
I see it coming. Dad kicks back a slug
of Beam. When Mom attacks, a rabid mink
in chenille houseshoes, Daddy disappears.

The Way Light Gets to Be

What your body ought to feel—
the lukewarm swish as a tongue's ideolect
murmurs: your furrows and tummy crease, every fold
of thigh or hip-dimple brimming with shadow.
The meat of us stiffens and swells, our human
skin bleeds honey and rose-bruise.
We kiss away the sheets, a linen field
that buries us like fallen children.
When God speaks He scratches
commandments into the freckled flesh

you wear like a distant day on the Pont Neuf,
or a Sam Cooke song in deep blue drizzle.
You dress this way to keep the light at bay,
that photo-degenerate carving the oncological surface.
Even Mona Lisa's fifteenth-century aura,
her skim of dancing photons, ripples, lured
like a soul by the sun's grand camera.
The wet world calls us too, of course: the vernal
surge of crocus bulbs, soft shoots of fuzz-buttoned
pussy-willow, dogwood's snow-burst

petal-shiver pasted to a rainy sidewalk's frieze.
Bulge and seepage, drip and thrust, each tumescent
fungus, every resinous milk-stemmed weed
that roots for nitrogen, the rock-fed lichen
doodling its millipartite portraiture: the Virgin Mother
scrawled across a streamside limestone sheet
torn by scrambling paws of crawdad-rustlers.
The swarm that feeds and replicates awaits
our death. Every glistening image listens
for breath-taking light's uneasy stir.

A kind of anesthetic to the daily
miracle keeps us plodding.
My father lies in the antiseptic heart
of a hospital, under a rubber mask and a local,
hears each stainless scratch, the scooping
of his eyeball jelly, the laser's focused hum.
The round world his retinal wall gathers
is underexposed, expiration date unclear.
Last summer, in Mexico City with Alex,
I chewed the stubborn rubber of tacos de ojo de vaca,

like gnawing a golf-ball's banded innards. The eye
is tougher than it looks. And, as any chi-chi
observer of popular culture could tell us,
has nearly no taste. The doctor sends my father home
with a silicone buckle, a guitar, and a tin cup.
This Zen-like notion of a detached retina—
as though the bond that binds to us oceans
of lilacs, phosphorus sea lips
drawling our languorous hours
over the vacant sand, was not our business

but only that of light—a macula receptor
blindly processing empty gesture, a vain
evolution unwinding that stupid helix
of the visible. You awaken,
fingers, hair—your eyes plaqued with matter.
And here, we rub and taste and burn our soft
hides together, a fleeting spark against the pitch.
Into one another, we curl
frightful shadows, the spindled film of our own
blank days, everything we love.

The August Patio

Such things my mother knew: how humid summer
spread a quilt across the alfalfa fields
at night, or why cicadas screeched their rumor

after the sun lay buried in the ground.
I knew nothing. Shy of kindergarten,
but long susceptible to faith, I stood

below the cusp of Leo and the virgin.
And on our patio, beneath the plum-wash
nightfall's looming flood, the constellations

loosing their silver stories in the hushed
heavens older than the speech of men,
Mother quietly began a splash

of poetry, her modest declamation
for the namesake of the redbrick school
I'd soon attend, half-days, in the autumn.

"Little Orphant Annie," and the hell-
bound children borne away by grinning goblins:
unstylish now, but Riley knew to tell

a story that compels a child to listen,
and Mother, her shadowed face leaning closer
through her voice, her star-spanked eyes glistening

into my stark thrall, was turning something over—
the way words lick our lips, the way they shape
our lives. The way she loved, with every quaver

and growl, each stiff hair on my tight nape,
the goblin's rasp, my startled nightbird chirp.

Visiting a River Valley Town

>One law shall be to him that is homeborn, and unto
>the stranger that sojourneth among you.
>—*Exodus 12.49*

Along the murky Verdigris, locust pods
rust and rattle autumn's umber plunge.
A troop of Brownies crunch through drying weeds.

The small zoo's prize-breeding pair of bison
forage prairie hay and tender acorns,
the patchy wool they shed in scraps all summer

thickens with October and the flies' last hurrah.
Near a canvas-covered carousel,
heart-shaped leaves collect in brittle heaps,

cupped in the yellowing park's deserted bandshell.
Presbyterian bells scour the air
while a pair of groundsmen spar with clippers,

trimming back a wild mulberry hedge.
The school that spanked me as a child, Orphan
Annie's school, James Whitcomb Riley

Elementary, has taken its red bricks
and disappeared. Like William Inge's picnic,
or Abel, our first monkey astronaut,

I do not live here any more. And though
the library fans its brass revolving doors
open to me, the brown-eyed lady checking

books no longer approves my reading. At dusk,
a red-haired boy in coonskin cap and freckles
pedals down the walk. His heavy, rust-pocked

Western Flyer squawks. That he may drift
like smoke above life's troubled lawns, I shape
the riffling wind to fit his hands. I shoot him

a dalliance of girls whose fruit-smudged lips
once pursed, disturbed beneath the shading elms.
They will not come this way again, and I,

pushed by urgencies that drive the leaves,
must catch the last train whistle echoing west.

Rebekah Orders Lasagna

At every church, or at most of them, they dug deep trenches, down to the waterline, wide and deep, depending on how large the parish was. And those who were responsible for the dead carried them on their backs in the night in which they died and threw them into the ditch, or else they paid a high price to those who would do it for them. The next morning, if there were many [bodies] in the trench, they covered them over with dirt. And then more bodies were put on top of them, with a little more dirt over those; they put layer on layer just like one puts layers of cheese in a lasagna.

—Marchione di Coppo Stefani
Cronaca fiorentina

Our starlet-eyed Rebekah, blonde, just
Home for the summer and faintly menacing,
Will not have it any other way:
Her mother (sprung from a long Norwegian line)
Must set aside the wash and make her famous
Lasagna, spinach salad and homemade bread.
So Cathy spreads the noodles in their greased
Glass pan, pats them with her fingertips
And curls their edges up. Now it's time
To spread the meat, a spicy Calabrese
Sausage, braised in olive oil, leeks,
Oregano, black pepper, a garlic smear.
Half-coagulated sauce-tomatoes
Redden the pan, the drift of cinnamon

I sneak into the mix, a pinch of salt.
"Italian afterbirth!" our youngest, Alex,
Returning from rehearsing Romeo
And Juliet, exults. As Gregory,
He's taken to Italian ways: the foods,
The feuds, the wise-guy cracking smart. Finished
With the final layer, Cathy sprinkles
Ricotta, lets a last drizzle of sauce
Dress the Pyrex sarcophagus she slides,
With a little prayer to her thrift-store wind-up timer,
Into the oven. And then my mother, bearing
A rhubarb pie like a swaddled babe in the crotch
Of her elbow, pokes her head through the broken backdoor
Screen, then sniffs with a gourmand's knowing air

And tells us that she's just this week discovered
A little restaurant that serves "The very
Best lasagna that I've ever tasted."
She doesn't catch her veiled insult, but does
Say Cathy's kitchen smells "sooo good. Just like
My mother's, on Sundays after services"—
Cathy, bent before the stove, twists and shoots
Me a dagger from over her shoulder, like a circus knife-
Trick artist. She loves my mom, but worries what
She'll say. I wonder where this sin will fall
In the grand scheme of their misunderstandings.
"It's my father's recipe," Cat snips,
"With any luck it will suffice for us."
Mother tries to patch things up. "I only

Meant," she frowns, "the best café lasagna."
So Mom, like Whitman, contradicts herself,
And I am left to ponder the marsalla
Odors wafting through my granny's kitchen.
You see, I don't recall a bit of this,
Just Granny's Midwest meatloaf, pan-fried chicken
And instant mashed potatoes. Did we ever
Eat Italian food? I chalk it up
To someone's wishful thinking, but remember
Granny armed with serving spoons, her splattered
Apron an armor she deployed against
A host of enemies—chopped beets or gravy-stains,
A splash of grease, the milk my brother spilled,
Predictable as Mussolini's trains;

Or Granddad mining his Hebrew dictionary:
He preached the ancient texts each Sunday, twice,
And lathered up the etymologists
Who jammed his small-town Presbyterian church.
Mother brought him home when she was six,
Elected him her daddy. That was that.
Sometimes I think about her other father,
The one who looked like me, who left his wife
And child in 'twenty-nine to Hoover's mercy—
Gramps, the one I met just once, age three
I'd guess, a wompus man in the Missouri woods,
Fresh from a six month bit in Joliet:
Murder Two—he'd pistol-whipped a black man
Over a poker game in East St. Louis,

Split his skull—but all I can recall
Is Grandpa handing me a stale Moon Pie.
So we all scoot our wobbly flesh-toned chairs
Up to our table, three generations stacked
In our own cheesy bonds. Across town,
At the Gardens of Memory, a pair of workers
Fresh from Guanajuato rest against
Their shovels, duck the gaze a huge Carrera-
Marble Jesus fans, disconsolate,
Across the measured sameness of the tombs.
They dig the holes here deeper, for double-decker
Vaults, in which the matrimonial dead
Lie one above the other, as in bunks,
Not side by side like lovers in one bed.

Our youngest burns his fingers on the grate
That holds the bread, but keeps himself composed
And juggles buttered loaves into the basket
"Like God deals battered lives into the casket."
In eighth grade World History, the Plague
Is all the rage: Black Death: a tattooed drum
And guitar band who digitally market
Their tattered denim fashions, studded belts
And low-end nose-rings turning dollar-green.
They slump around and pose as though their pallid
Ennui could be terminal. Alex
Thinks he'll start a next-wave band. Red Flea.
He tells us "Ring Around the Rosy" stems
From plague-lore, plans to play it loud, with drums.

He also wants to know where Sputnik's hiding.
Rebekah's college boyfriend, Sputnik seems
A youth who's doomed, like poems, to loss and desire:
Rebekah goes through men like I use tires.
We'd call him Nick, his given name, but we
Already have a Nick, and anyway,
Sputnik studies at the astronaut
Academy, where moony students read,
And knows the names of all the layers of air—
The atmo-, strato-, tropo-, hoodoo-spheres
Of scientific baklava we breathe:
A science like the phylo dough our names
Encode, enveloping the nuts and honey
Of the families we're gravely born

35

Into, perhaps amend. Cathy guesses
Sputnik's orbiting the house, his Ford
Another aging Mir with burned-out brakes;
But frankly, we all feel a little nervous.
He comes from Girl Scout Camp, a carrier
Of mononucleosis, the plague of teenage
Girls (a lifeguard, he perches over the lake
And scans bikinied thirteen-year-old babes
With surplus-store binoculars—confused
As that Carrera-marble Christ). Rebekah
Greets these innuendoes with unveiled
Contempt and the worst insult she knows: "Boys!"
"We only want what's best for her," they plead,
But no one's buying that. We bow for grace.

Cathy shifts her role from cook to host,
Starts the bread around while I uncork
A frisky Carmignano, young and ruby-red,
To lubricate our tongues. Of all of us,
Cathy knows the trick to calm Rebekah.
"What is an innuendo?" Cathy asks,
Then laughs, "An Italian enema!"
Our forks poised halfway to our open mouths,
Nick, who studies Medieval History
At the local college, trumps his funny mother,
Announcing that he's digested the Marchione
Di Coppo Stefani's *Testimonio*,
How the poorest poor tossed plague-racked corpses
Into ditches trenched around each church . . .

As with one common eye we see them, stacked
In our lasagna: the buboed Florentines,
Scarf-wrapped Mamas, aunts engulfed in meat-sauce,
The uncorrupted children newly orphaned
And left to tend their pustulating sores,
Black-egg swellings suppurating groin
And armpit; the lung-racked panderers, the bleeding
Prostitutes who never lay this still
So near the Church. The oldest black-ragged crones
Who outlived their descendants, stumbling under
Faggot bundles, bearing fuel from empty
Hearth to empty hearth until, exhausted,
They simply fall and do not rise again.
Witches with their failing medicines—

36

Yarrow, mandrake, powdered amanita.
Or youthful painters, their fledgling perspective lost
In a Byzantine maze of mystics, gypsies and Jews—
At every door, another unclean host.
Horseflesh fouls the street; the stricken pets,
The lunatics set loose to hemorrhage,
Reminiscent of those fierce condotierri
Boiled to tempest in the feudal teapots—
Mother's seen enough, and raps Nick's head
With her sausaged fork. Rebekah leaps from her chair,
"Mom, make him stop. I can't stomach
A thing now." I'm surprised that Nick has read
So widely out of text—but Cathy will not
Brook my pleasure now. "Stop," I bark.

The sedimentary dead who fell to buttress
Up the church may just as well have died
In different eons—lutists, lovers, liars,
They mark their status by their strata, like mollusks,
Or dinosaurs. The first to die, thrown nearest
Hell's warm grates, will spread their soul-fired wings,
Rapturous, and sail on Jesu's breath
Where even Sputnik's rocket cannot follow,
While their neighbors chew a last night's mud.
But high in the Apennines, a Bishop dodges
Death— a clearing in the beechwoods where his
Scared attendants work a tree-rigged fan
In shifts to blow the vapors from His Person.
Lancing down from Heaven, a shaft of sunshine

Anoints the tonsured workers. They wash in holy
Water, drive the frightened peasants down
The hill with halberds: His Holiness bends to your prayers;
You must redeem your families, go hence!
And bear your dead to final victory.
Meanwhile, back at the Gardens of Memory,
Enrique and Reynaldo have forgotten
Their lunches at home and drive for a Taco Bell
Burrito: the seven-layer. Gringo-food, they laugh.
We finish up our food and lave the dishes.
Sputnik rinses, Rebekah gives advice
And chides him teasingly for coming late.
He got the street directions backwards. "You'll
Never find the moon," she remonstrates,

Then takes a cell-phone call from brother Neil,
Who's moved to Santa Barbara, a beach-
Bound scholar surfing to a PhD
In Sociology. He reads no French,
But cites Lacan and Derrida as if
They were the men who peddle Meals-on-Wheels
From door to door across the barrio:
A sociology of doubt and want.
He's called to lure his baby sister west,
Out of the family's close-quartered orbit:
Hollywood! The Pasadena Playhouse!
Reality T.V.! Our little solar
System feels another tug from Beyond.
I tap my heart for those already gone.

After lunch we visit Walden, Cat's dad.
He rests in a Home, where he expresses nothing
We can bring ourselves to understand.
His mind spins like an Osterizer blender,
A whirl of memories a step removed
From any life of his that we remember.
A top-rank culinary innovator,
He was head chef at Guido's Place, but now
He's lost without his prime ingredients:
Us. Or are we really that important?
Each of us a layer of fresh lasagna—
Pasta, cheese, or meat, we play our parts—
But he can never really catch the taste
Until we've all been thoroughly chewed up.

We do not know that one more year will fetch
Walden back home. A broken hip. We'll rent
A bed, hydraulic, to park in the dining room
For easy access—lay him where the table
Used to stand. We'll touch him, squeeze him water
From a sponge; he won't speak, but rattle
Deep down in his lungs. Cathy's song,
A tear-brimmed "Old Dan Tucker," will earn a smile,
But morphine rubs us out, a family
Who could be anyone—his grandparents,
Perhaps, or boyhood baseball players. We'll catch
In a familiar pose around the bed,
Each of us in our accustomed place
At the vanished table, bereft of wine or bread.

Lovebirds and Other Fish

and sprinkled dust upon their heads toward heaven
Job 2.12

The Shallows

Shall I say your mouth unfolds around sleep
the way a harbor bays its foggy moan
to sloops, a tune that salt exhales through foam,
the slough of kelp across a rocky beach?

Flotsam and Jetsam your father used to call us,
spun in the eddies of our backwater desires—
but now our parents swim beneath the grass,
the rustle of their gills a distant music

murmuring across the empty years
till we ourselves, grown pliable and soft,
are borne like spume in a flood, our fragile bodies
floating as bubbles, a delicate debris,

to lie, mute fossils buried in the chalk.
The bed we ride to sleep once rocked the sea—
and we a pair of ichthyosaurs, dim beasts
feeding in the shallows of each other.

What the Loon Believes

The humid redolence of shadows
gathers, shade by shade, until we echo
in a dove's call, an owl's murmur, radiance
strolling the river at dusk. This is not
our first trip, timing the ripples

feeding perch strike against the surface
of this blue, your mortal appetite
smelling of willow and sedge.
What if a fire-scorched birch, black as imagination,
charms those people we never made

time to become? Will these lavender
weed-tips at wood's edge grieve,
or thrill to the mutual fading
of our paired sexes? White wings
blaze beneath the canopy of leaves,

then vanish, lost and silent as light.
The nascent constellations glimmer,
pale ornaments strung through elm and elder.
Along this bank walk weightlessness,
suspension, our two bodies buoyed

between dozens of atmospheres.
Quivering between poor faith and clumsy works,
we struggle, gifted with the word
that shivers, numinous, across calm water.
If you are egret, I am a loon.

We egg each other on,
starting over, casual as friends
against the skin, pale feet sunk in mud,
and I rehearse my error, believing
in one thing a woman knows.

Lot's Daughters

Genesis 19

Our sweethearts thought that Daddy's escape tip
Was quite a joke—that he who would have turned
His virgin daughters—us!—(overripe,
Perhaps, but trothed in law and nearly dowered)
Over to a crowd of het-up perverts
Eager for a taste of angel ass
Was himself given to humor. Now they're converts—
Blown like all the Sodomites to glass
Or salt. And Mother got what she most craved,
A licking every night from desert beasts
Who need her salt, not just some depraved
Satisfaction. They tongue her till she's creased.
And Daddy nips his wineskin, seeds each furrow
As he toils, nightly, here in our burrow.

King's Harlot to Rook One

I Kings 3.16-28

I look the hell I've lived, and no longer bluff
So easily as some. But, I can say
King David's son's as wise an ass as any
Crowned and mantled ninny who broods a rough
Throneful of daily problematic stuff.
I see through his ploy, but the "little lady,"
A kohl-eyed strumpet in wool-nap rudely
Bawling at his proposition (his own laugh
Barely suppressed) (we call him "Solemn man,"
But wink——he sports with Ammonites!), bleats
Beneath his knife like a sacrificial lamb.
This ram-horn king would cleave her kinky pelt
A thousand times before he'd halve a damn
Citizen. Her child drooled on the rug. I split.

What the Table-dancer Earned

Matthew 14.1-13; Mark 6.16-29

John was madder than a hornet, Mother
Said, and stuck his nose too deeply where
It didn't belong. Simply put, he bugged her.

Got beneath her skin. Chastised Uncle
("Rapping the ruler's knuckles" I heard him chuckle)
Herod once too often—over that cuckold

Business he put Mother through with Dad.
Anyway, Mother says John ate insects—and she'd
Designed the coolest plan to bite his head

Off, just like any spider, with me as web-wriggling
Bait! When Uncle urged me to dance and sing
For the big-wigs, he was plastered and offered me anything.

—Anything! I stared at Mom. "Gold would be adequate,"
I mouthed, but nooo. "John's head," she hissed. "On a plate."

Circus Girl

Beasts, ubiquitous and available, swagger
   before the succulent, ambrosial years.

Spots alternate with stripes and the entire
   fur-bearing world sleeps with the aid

of generous machines; serendipity
   proves no watchword,

and this suspension between the air
   and its unspeakable resting place

could be true impressionism, a hint
   of decay in the breeze charging the light,

oppressive mist. Some people dress
   in pineapples and orchids. In the elephant

dirt, they trip on tangled tightropes
   while slack-jawed spotlights reckon

every swiveling face that clowns their fall.
   She sets out wheat and sunflowers

in a pale green bowl
   for her tigers, gruel for the tubas.

Indulgences

A powder of light scatters from the water like mist—
like the palsied hand, scarred silver with necrosis,
that charted our ticklish route along the bayou
from an unclean bed. And we who float
engulfed in radiance, blind to the raucous

shorebirds, deaf to the effulgence that quiets
our carping lines, scull across the surface
as if borne on bush-league faith and wish ourselves
to rise beyond our skin and wash our griefs
like astral fishers in the gulls' ancestral cries.

So we were not the ones to find her, nestled,
a rotting log among the salt-shanked roots
where turtles grind their beaks on bone, mince
discarded babes, lost slaves, the innocents
who envy us the nets we drag through shallows.

The paper gave her age as twelve, "colored,
of good family," who paled in the livid shadows
moonwash weaves beneath the cypress leaves
and the black mangrove, who dived as if she'd love
to wear the rictic alligator's hide.

How Domenica Lazzari Survives on Light

Witnesses attest that Lazzari's stigmata bled every Friday from the time of their first appearance through her death in 1848, at the age of 33, and that she herself lived without food, subsisting only on Holy Communion.

Her stigmatized hands cup into the brash
well of it, and she laps at lazy red
strontium, violet potassium,

verdant hum of barium.
Indifferent to substance itself, she transmits

the radiant joy of her Christ,
spectral, ethereal, attentive,
the length of her passion's waves.

Her knees open to prepossessing stone,
she flays her back to scarlet tatters,

drains her perfumed wounds
before the reliquary as taut prayer twists,
colors the spectrographic lines, shrinks

those blind regions where hunger urges
and bends her to a bacchanal of light.

The Bee of Hearts

How he hovers, nimbly sips
a draught from every weed and flower
ranged along my garden's border—
zinnia, larkspur, a splash of tulips—
and how he zips

from lavender to daffodil
like a sprinter on the make,
a cloud of pollen in his wake
after he has drunk his fill.
As chlorophyll

transubstantiates the sun
to protein, so this bustling bee
turns blossoms into food for me:
I feed wherever nectar runs:
a little bun,

a little knife, a honeyed picnic
in the arbor with my wife, —
her calf-mad eye! My passion rife!
We murmur love-talk low and manic,
our faces rictic

with delight as bees dart in
and bees dart out—as jonquils toss
their heads about. We lie on moss
as delicate and soft as satin
and buzz with sin.

And one bee watches, one bee knows
how we mount and ride each other,
spur each other into lather;
from our tongue-tips to our toes
we spark and glow.

Now we repose, a pair of sweethearts
on the felt-green floor of spring
where the tallywhackers sing
of April's bee-prick, where we chart
the bee of hearts.

Honey
> Then there's the sound a vow makes when it shatters
> —*Bruce Bond*

Our old terrier would soil the divan, but we don't
harbor any old terriers, and our clean couch,
short and rigidly uncomfortable, may be more
properly termed a love-seat. Out in that world
where people meet for paychecks, beer, and slow-pitch

softball, love blows out her forty candles
and a brush of pollen sullens on moist skin.
This is the way we planned it: our elder in-laws
die, or wrap themselves in the gauze
of an impossible past, arteries sludged

with all they wished for us, as if they ever thought
of us as anything but unrelenting youth
accumulating layers of adipose. Our daughter
follows her body into adolescence, trails
a tumescent line of swains across the fading carpet—

the last blue-jeaned spasms of electricity
before the television signals us to silence
and communion: O spirit-eye who pries
our hearts to advertise, turn us from reverie
in obedience. A knock at the door. We flinch,

arise to answer, in a worn-out vernacular,
the oldest visitor of all. And out beyond her
shoulder, the landscape starts to flicker, the patient
shrubbery eases out of its skin, becomes a breath
where bees linger at twilight, listening for honey.

The Kites

> All flesh is not the same flesh: but there is one kind of flesh of men, another flesh of beasts, another of fishes, and another of birds.
> —*I Corinthians 15.39*

These birds breed in juvenile plumage,
like us, avid after the first
molt, at the first feathery touch.
With half-closed wings
one stoops, talons a water-rat

from the bank's green verge,
absconds to a twig nest, raddled,
crow-fashion, in the tree's top fork.
She chippers at her young,
their buff down newly fletched,

as we sit, resting from our hike
along the hedgerows to the Medicine
River and the rusted Chinaberry
from which this pair of kites flash
like two scimitars. The nestlings clamor,

gray bills rollicking above
the rookery's walnut leaf doublure.
Soon, the male plummets, then wheels
to catch an updraft. With each dive
he falls nearer to us,

black eyes staring from black
mask. As we rise and walk,
we part the ripe wheat panicles,
raise a small cicada cloud.
Shearing the air like a boomerang,

he eats their shattered abdomens
in flight. Our insoles lined with stones,
we beat the field like half-wit saints
to feed this dour angel whose plaits
we can't unravel, can't embrace.

Waiting

> neither budding nor fading, /Not in the scheme of generation
> —T.S. Eliot

How, peregrine, will you come
to our small town? Like a shuttlecock
bouncing between our sweltering atmospheres?
A bead on the macadam string
that binds us one to another,
leaving your sere yellow grasses
to visit our chert-pocked hills, our gnarled hedgerows
fierce with the thorns our flint-chapped Lord
adorns with his hard sufferance? We fail
in our voluptuousness, little knowing
how we fail, as if your rough kingship,
hailing the pigs from the road, stirring
the highway dust, confounds the parched hours
of our own laceration.

Will you find us, when you come,
waiting as cows on a ridge-spine, bovine
in our gratitude, purposeful only
in our repose? May you astonish us—
your tongue ignite the salt-block
like an ember, the sea of grass
to flame—your blade christen our leather shoulders.
Bleak invalids, we pray in ruined churches,
cough the awful host like a hairball
clutched in our throats. Thus transpires the season
of common wind. Of barns knuckling under.
Of compliance and refining fire.

Vernal Equinox

Turning the corner down to the market,
in love with myself, I smile as the laughing
sparrows slap their knees, their shrill notes
clamorous on the telephone wire, scaled
feet tickled by giggled love-talk as their auras
flame through the common atmosphere.

Passing a wire fence strangled
with honeysuckle, I smell the truth
that some things simply cannot be revealed.
Because I live in "The Air Capitol of the World"
a noisy little airplane often buzzes overhead.

Today, it grumbles a rip-saw shadow across me,
but flashes, in fact, its cheery single-engine blue
with amaryllis trim. The little Cessna sports
a big number on its tail, which makes me think
that perhaps dogs should too, drawing
my attention, in turn, to a striped tabby cat

lurking beneath my neighbor's juniper tree.
Should I purchase a canary?
blue or yellow? I can't decide
and go to calculating the cost of seed.
Things start looking good when I realize
I don't subscribe to the newspaper.

Herds of pastel automobiles bleat
their sheepish compliments as I whistle my way
across the street, hands a'pocket, that crazy
sun making chlorophyll everywhere,
but none for me, dapper in a straw hat

and a pink tint. What if the teenage
girl with the big pair falls
for me? With my balding pate and my pot
belly handsomely bobbing, do I not appear
European? If only I possessed a memory,
I could be like Proust! A Coca-Cola
and a jelly donut remind me of yesterday!

The History of Sleep
    Sleep opens within us an inn for phantoms

                                                      —*Gaston Bachelard*

1.
It hasn't worn the kind of clothes you'd wear
to snuggle in——bunny feet, drop panels——for years,

but often works all night in bib overalls.
Strung from double-stitched loops, tools dangle

over the sand-plugged eyes the world rubs tossing
from side to side——Beijing, New York, Beijing——

never settling, sloshing the ocean beds
like a colicky baby. Winkin blinks and nods.

2.
I know an all-night nurse who catches taxis
home at sun-up, falls in bed and passes

into something short of slumber. Last night
she lost another customer to that light

the dying see as they slam the door on pain,
turn away from mundane things like evergreen

sprays at Christmas, air-soled shoes, bug-
zappers, chilly nights in sleeping bags.

When this morning's rose-red burst of dawn
hits her like a heart attack, her bones

convulse to powder and the taxi driver
lends her a flurry of concern, then pours

her a cup of Joe from his thermos. It doesn't touch
the cold spot in her heart, cannot reach

the operation's failure, the frail gray body
trundled on its chrome-infected gurney.

She used to be a harder case, inured
to death and illness, the black rage of the injured.

A whistle calls the first-shift to their tools,
priests to their prayers, fools to other fools,

and the nightshift home to their unshaven lovers,
their sleeping pills and unrequited covers.

3.
I'm married to a vet. Twice. The chump
whiffed victory gas in a blown-up ammo dump

in south Iraq that's made him cranky, a plume
of hyper-toxic Babylonian fumes;

now he doctors animals—ferrets, goats,
the hundred mangy creatures children tote

home to parents. The world of wag-tails creeps
into his office; he puts stray cats to sleep.

I find him anything but boring. A kind
of Nazi expediency frames his mind,

and sleep, I think, is what he wishes for
himself above all other earthly pleasures,

but I won't let him go without a kiss
and one thing leads, as everybody says,

to another, until pretty soon it dawns on us
we've loved all night, like teenagers in lust.

As I drift, my head against his chest,
he swears I'm the cat's pajamas. I get no rest.

Canapés

Am I come to this, a starker age
when I relinquish mirrors, their bevels, their beauties,
their scars, their parties full of the loveliest
strangers—their ghastly, unknown solitary?

Am I now less than my vision? Risen like smoke
to the ceiling, floating around with the gossip, Dear,
struggling to find myself—and who in the crowd
will look for me beyond the chandelier?

I cloud, an abstract, hazy-blue suggestion.
Beneath me, the wine passes, and the canapés
glisten on their polished silver barges,
a cargo of small answers to a larger question.

Resolution

A rustle in dog-rose bramble. Did you build
a nest to ring our feathered bed?
You warble low as sweetpea Jesus, scarred

with me. Thistle-braided, bittersweet
as love's pierced flesh, you breathe each twist
of air into an art that resurrects

hard passion in our shrub. Though I've borne
the rugged twigs of your disdain
above the cat-crossed alleys and the lawns

where hired men shake their rakes and widows yawn
in concert with the mowers' moan,
shall we not find it lovelier to drown

at last in wanton song? Flicker, titmouse,
tucked thorn-thick in briar—how fast
the nettled rose that bleeds us folds us close.

And how the evening seizes us! Great hands
obscure our twilit song, descend
like beetling wings that glide to daylight's end.

Sordamente. Mute the tarnished brass
as we resolve to night, faceless,
destitute of flame or ardor, vast.

About the Author

John Jenkinson's misspent youth consisted of long years enduring low-end jobs – gandydancing, tin-man hustling, drumming, taxi-driving, grifting and gravesite peddling among them. A late return to the groves of Academe resulted in an MFA from Wichita State University, a PhD from the University of North Texas, and a Milton Center post-doctoral Fellowship in Poetry at Newman University. His most cherished degree, however, remains the one he earned at the School of Hard Knocks, where he continues post-graduate studies. John's poems have been the recipients of an AWP Intro Journals award, the Ellipses Prize, a New Voices Award, a Balticon Science Fiction Award, and awards from Kansas Voices. His poems appear in a surprising variety of journals and anthologies. Currently, he teaches literature and writing at Butler Community College in Kansas, where he advises the Chess Society and directs the Oil Hill Reading Series. John spends his spare time balancing four children, his fiction-writing wife Catherine Dryden, two cats and a dog – and has taken up song-writing.

Printed in the United States
42890LVS00006B/349-408